ECCLESIASTES WITH
GOD'S WISDOM

Navigate life wisely with 30+ quotes &
proverbs of wisdom from the Biblical
book of Ecclesiastes

By ML James

AUDIOBOOK OFFER

If you are new to Audible you can get the audiobook version of this book free with a free 30 days Audible trial.

Please follow the below *bit.ly* links based on where you reside.

US: *bit.ly/MLJ_Ecclesiastes_US*

UK: *bit.ly/MLJ_ Ecclesiastes_UK*

France: *bit.ly/MLJ_ Ecclesiastes_FR*

Germany: *bit.ly/MLJ_ Ecclesiastes_DE*

All other countries: *bit.ly/MLJ_Ecclesiastes_Others*

TABLE OF CONTENTS

INTRODUCTION

"Get good advice and you will succeed. Don't go charging into battle without a plan." Proverbs 20:18

- Seeking insights for living life wisely?
- Interested in learning & applying ancient time-tested wisdom?
- Know someone who might benefit from this?

This Christian wisdom literature contains 30+ quotes & proverbs of wisdom from the Biblical book of Ecclesiastes that can be great for anyone interested in living wisely.

It can empower, inspire & steer you to do so through:

- Ancient wisdom & instructions in wise dealing.
- Discerning the words of understanding.
- Giving shrewdness to the inexperienced.

- Knowledge and discretion to the young.
- Attaining sound counsel.

Get ready to see your life transform over time as you learn, meditate upon & apply the divine wisdom!

DEDICATION

This book is dedicated to my dad.

Dad's been my rock, speaking words of love & wisdom into my life. His words & life inspires, guides and directs my path.

Dad's encouragement to study the Biblical book of Ecclesiastes has lead me to write this book.

I love you dad.

30+ QUOTES & PROVERBS OF WISDOM

QUOTE #1

For everything there is a season, and a time for every purpose under heaven:

a time to be born, and a time to die;

a time to plant, and a time to pluck up that which is planted;

a time to break down, and a time to build up;

a time to weep, and a time to laugh;

a time to mourn, and a time to dance;

a time to cast away stones, and a time to gather stones together;

a time to embrace, and a time to refrain from embracing;

a time to seek, and a time to lose; a time to keep, and a time to cast away; a time to tear, and a time to sew;

a time to keep silence, and a time to speak; a time to love, and a time to hate;

a time for war, and a time for peace.

ECCLESIASTES 3:1-2, 4-8

LET'S REFLECT ON THE QUOTE & WRITE YOUR THOUGHTS

QUOTE #2

I returned, and saw under the sun, that the race is not to the swift, nor the battle to the strong, neither yet bread to the wise, nor yet riches to men of understanding, nor yet favor to men of skill; but time and chance happen to them all.

For man also doesn't know his time. As the fish that are taken in an evil net, and as the birds that are caught in the snare, even so are the sons of men snared in an evil time, when it falls suddenly on them.

I have also seen wisdom under the sun in this way, and it seemed great to me. There was a little city, and few men within it; and a great king came against it, besieged it, and built great siege works against it.

Now a poor wise man was found in it, and he by his wisdom delivered the city; yet no man remembered that same poor man.

Then said I, Wisdom is better than strength. Nevertheless the poor man's wisdom is despised, and his words are not heard.

The words of the wise heard in quiet are better than the cry of him who rules among fools. Wisdom is better than weapons of war; but one sinner destroys much good.

ECCLESIASTES 9:11-18

LET'S REFLECT ON THE QUOTE & WRITE YOUR THOUGHTS

QUOTE #3

It is good that you should take hold of this. Yes, also from that do not withdraw your hand; for he who fears God will come forth from them all.

Wisdom is a strength to the wise man more than ten rulers who are in a city. Surely there is not a righteous man on earth, who does good and doesn't sin.

Also do not take heed to all words that are spoken, lest you hear your servant curse you; for often your own heart knows that you yourself have likewise cursed others.

ECCLESIASTES 7:18-22

LET'S REFLECT ON THE QUOTE & WRITE YOUR THOUGHTS

QUOTE #4

Surely extortion makes the wise man foolish; and a bribe destroys the understanding. Better is the end of a thing than its beginning. The patient in spirit is better than the proud in spirit.

Do not be hasty in your spirit to be angry, for anger rests in the bosom of fools.

Do not say, "Why were the former days better than these?" For you do not ask wisely about this. Wisdom is as good as an inheritance. Yes, it is more excellent for those who see the sun.

For wisdom is a defense, even as money is a defense; but the excellency of knowledge is that wisdom preserves the life of him who has it.

Consider the work of God, for who can make that straight, which he has made crooked?

In the day of prosperity be joyful, and in the day of adversity consider; yes, God has made the one side by side with the other, to the end that man should not find out anything after him.

ECCLESIASTES 7:7-14

LET'S REFLECT ON THE QUOTE & WRITE YOUR THOUGHTS

_____
_____
_____
_____
_____
_____
_____
_____
_____
_____
_____
_____
_____
_____
_____
_____
_____
_____
_____
_____
_____
_____
_____
_____
_____
_____

QUOTE #5

God has made everything beautiful in its time. I know that there is nothing better for man than to rejoice, and to do good as long as they live. Also that every man should eat and drink, and enjoy good in all his labor, is the gift of God.

I know that whatever God does, it shall be forever. Nothing can be added to it, nor anything taken from it; and God has done it, that men should fear before him.

That which is has been long ago, and that which is to be has been long ago: and God seeks again that which is passed away.

ECCLESIASTES 3:11-15

LET'S REFLECT ON THE QUOTE & WRITE YOUR THOUGHTS

QUOTE #6

Remember also your Creator in the days of your youth, before the evil days come, and the years draw near, when you will say, "I have no pleasure in them;"

Before the sun, the light, the moon, and the stars are darkened, and the clouds return after the rain; in the day when the keepers of the house shall tremble, and the strong men shall bow themselves, and the grinders cease because they are few, and those who look out of the windows are darkened, and the doors shall be shut in the street;

When the sound of the grinding is low, and one shall rise up at the voice of a bird, and all the daughters of music shall be brought low;

Also, they are afraid of heights, and of terrors in the way; and the almond tree blossoms, and the grasshopper is burdened, and the caper bush fails;

Because man goes to his everlasting home, and the mourners go about the streets: before the silver cord is severed, or the golden bowl is broken, or the pitcher is broken at the spring, or the wheel broken at the cistern, and the dust returns to the earth as it was, and the spirit returns to God who gave it.

ECCLESIASTES 12:1-7

LET'S REFLECT ON THE QUOTE & WRITE YOUR THOUGHTS

QUOTE #7

Though a sinner commits crimes a hundred times, and lives long, yet surely I know that it will be better with those who fear God, who are reverent before him.

But it shall not be well with the wicked, neither shall he lengthen days like a shadow; because he doesn't fear God.

ECCLESIASTES 8:12-13

LET'S REFLECT ON THE QUOTE & WRITE YOUR THOUGHTS

QUOTE #8

He who digs a pit may fall into it; and whoever breaks through a wall may be bitten by a serpent.

Whoever carves out stones may be injured by them. Whoever splits wood may be endangered thereby.

If the axe is blunt, and one doesn't sharpen the edge, then he must use more strength; but skill brings success.

If the serpent bites before it is charmed, then is there no profit for the charmer's tongue.

The words of a wise man's mouth are gracious; but a fool is swallowed by his own lips. The beginning of the words of his mouth is foolishness; and the end of his talk is mischievous madness.

A fool also multiplies words. Man doesn't know what will be; and that which will be after him, who can tell him?

ECCLESIASTES 10:8-14

LET'S REFLECT ON THE QUOTE & WRITE YOUR THOUGHTS

QUOTE #9

Rejoice, young man, in your youth, and let your heart cheer you in the days of your youth, and walk in the ways of your heart, and in the sight of your eyes; but know that for all these things God will bring you into judgment.

Therefore remove sorrow from your heart, and put away evil from your flesh; for youth and the dawn of life are vanity.

ECCLESIASTES 11:9-10

LET'S REFLECT ON THE QUOTE & WRITE YOUR THOUGHTS

QUOTE #10

A good name is better than fine perfume; and the day of death better than the day of one's birth. It is better to go to the house of mourning than to go to the house of feasting: for that is the end of all men, and the living should take this to heart.

Sorrow is better than laughter; for by the sadness of the face the heart is made good. The heart of the wise is in the house of mourning; but the heart of fools is in the house of mirth.

It is better to hear the rebuke of the wise, than for a man to hear the song of fools. For as the crackling of thorns under a pot, so is the laughter of the fool. This also is vanity.

ECCLESIASTES 7:1-6

LET'S REFLECT ON THE QUOTE & WRITE YOUR THOUGHTS

QUOTE #11

I turned around, and my heart sought to know and to search out, and to seek wisdom and the scheme of things, and to know that wickedness is stupidity, and that foolishness is madness.

I find more bitter than death the woman whose heart is snares and traps, whose hands are chains. Whoever pleases God shall escape from her; but the sinner will be ensnared by her.

ECCLESIASTES 7:25-26

LET'S REFLECT ON THE QUOTE & WRITE YOUR THOUGHTS

_____
_____
_____
_____
_____
_____
_____
_____
_____
_____
_____
_____
_____
_____
_____
_____
_____
_____
_____
_____
_____

QUOTE #12

In the morning sow your seed, and in the evening do not withhold your hand; for you do not know which will prosper, whether this or that, or whether they will both be equally good.

Truly the light is sweet, and a pleasant thing it is for the eyes to see the sun. Yes, if a man lives many years, let him rejoice in them all; but let him remember the days of darkness, for they shall be many. All that comes is vanity.

ECCLESIASTES 11:6-8

LET'S REFLECT ON THE QUOTE & WRITE YOUR THOUGHTS

QUOTE #13

There is one who is alone, and he has neither son nor brother. There is no end to all of his labor, neither are his eyes satisfied with wealth.

For whom then, do I labor, and deprive my soul of enjoyment? This also is vanity, yes, it is a miserable business. Two are better than one, because they have a good reward for their labor.

For if they fall, the one will lift up his fellow; but woe to him who is alone when he falls, and doesn't have another to lift him up. Again, if two lie together, then they have warmth; but how can one keep warm alone?

If a man prevails against one who is alone, two shall withstand him; and a threefold cord is not quickly broken.

Better is a poor and wise youth than an old and foolish king who doesn't know how to receive admonition any more. For out of prison he came forth to be king; yes, even in his kingdom he was born poor.

ECCLESIASTES 4:8-14

LET'S REFLECT ON THE QUOTE & WRITE YOUR THOUGHTS

_____
_____
_____
_____
_____
_____
_____
_____
_____
_____
_____
_____
_____
_____
_____
_____
_____
_____
_____
_____
_____
_____

QUOTE #14

For to the man who pleases God, God gives wisdom, knowledge, and joy; but to the sinner he gives travail, to gather and to heap up, that he may give to him who pleases God. This also is vanity and a chasing after wind.

ECCLESIASTES 2:26

LET'S REFLECT ON THE QUOTE & WRITE YOUR THOUGHTS

QUOTE #15

I made myself great works. I built myself houses. I planted myself vineyards. I made myself gardens and parks, and I planted trees in them of all kinds of fruit.

I made myself pools of water, to water from it the forest where trees were reared. I bought male servants and female servants, and had servants born in my house.

I also had great possessions of herds and flocks, above all who were before me in Jerusalem; I also gathered silver and gold for myself, and the treasure of kings and of the provinces.

I got myself male and female singers, and the delights of the sons of men – musical instruments, and that of all sorts.

So I was great, and increased more than all who were before me in Jerusalem. My wisdom also remained with me.

Whatever my eyes desired, I did not keep from them. I did not withhold my heart from any joy, for my heart rejoiced because of all my labor, and this was my portion from all my labor.

Then I looked at all the works that my hands had worked, and at the labor that I had labored to do; and look, all was vanity and a chasing after wind, and there was no profit under the sun.

ECCLESIASTES 2:4-11

LET'S REFLECT ON THE QUOTE & WRITE YOUR THOUGHTS

QUOTE #16

I said in my heart, "God will judge the righteous and the wicked; for there is a time there for every purpose and for every work."

I said in my heart, "As for the sons of men, God tests them, so that they may see that they themselves are like animals. For that which happens to the sons of men happens to animals. Even one thing happens to them.

As the one dies, so the other dies. Yes, they have all one breath; and man has no advantage over the animals: for all is vanity. All go to one place. All are from the dust, and all turn to dust again."

ECCLESIASTES 3:17-20

LET'S REFLECT ON THE QUOTE & WRITE YOUR THOUGHTS

QUOTE #17

The words of the wise are like goads; and like nails well fastened are words from the masters of collections, which are given from one shepherd.

Furthermore, my son, be admonished: of making many books there is no end; and much study is a weariness of the flesh.

This is the end of the matter. All has been heard. Fear God, and keep his commandments; for this is the whole duty of man.

For God will bring every work into judgment, with every hidden thing, whether it is good, or whether it is evil.

ECCLESIASTES 12:11-14

LET'S REFLECT ON THE QUOTE & WRITE YOUR THOUGHTS

QUOTE #18

What does man gain from all his labor in which he labors under the sun? One generation goes, and another generation comes; but the earth remains forever. The sun also rises, and the sun goes down, and hurries to its place where it rises.

The wind goes toward the south, and turns around to the north. It turns around continually as it goes, and the wind returns again to its courses.

All the rivers run into the sea, yet the sea is not full. To the place where the rivers flow, there they flow again.

All things are full of weariness beyond uttering. The eye is not satisfied with seeing, nor the ear filled with hearing.

That which has been is that which shall be; and that which has been done is that which shall be done: and there is no new thing under the sun. Is there a thing of which it may be said, "Look, this is new?"

It has been long ago, in the ages which were before us. There is no memory of the former; neither shall there be any memory of the latter that are to come, among those that shall come after.

ECCLESIASTES 1:3-11

LET'S REFLECT ON THE QUOTE & WRITE YOUR THOUGHTS

QUOTE #19

The sleep of a laboring man is sweet, whether he eats little or much; but the abundance of the rich will not allow him to sleep.

ECCLESIASTES 5:12

LET'S REFLECT ON THE QUOTE & WRITE YOUR THOUGHTS

QUOTE #20

I turned myself to consider wisdom, madness, and folly. For what can the man who comes after the king do? Just that which he has already done.

Then I saw that wisdom excels folly, as far as light excels darkness. The wise man's eyes are in his head, and the fool walks in darkness — and yet I perceived that one event happens to them all.

ECCLESIASTES 2:12-14

LET'S REFLECT ON THE QUOTE & WRITE YOUR THOUGHTS

QUOTE #21

Then I saw all the labor and achievement that is the envy of a man's neighbor. This also is vanity and a striving after wind.

The fool folds his hands together and ruins himself. Better is a handful, with quietness, than two handfuls with labor and chasing after wind.

ECCLESIASTES 4:4-6

LET'S REFLECT ON THE QUOTE & WRITE YOUR THOUGHTS

QUOTE #22

Guard your step when you go to the house of God. To draw near to listen is better than to give the sacrifice of fools, for they do not know that they do evil.

Do not be rash with your mouth, and do not let your heart be hasty to utter anything before God; for God is in heaven, and you on earth. Therefore let your words be few.

For as a dream comes with a multitude of cares, so a fool's speech with a multitude of words. When you vow a vow to God, do not defer to pay it; for he has no pleasure in fools. Pay that which you vow.

It is better that you should not vow, than that you should vow and not pay. Do not allow your mouth to lead you into sin. Do not protest before the messenger that this was a mistake.

Why should God be angry at your voice, and destroy the work of your hands? For in the multitude of dreams there are vanities, as well as in many words: but you must fear God.

If you see the oppression of the poor, and the violent taking away of justice and righteousness in a district, do not marvel at the matter.

ECCLESIASTES 5:1-8

LET'S REFLECT ON THE QUOTE & WRITE YOUR THOUGHTS

QUOTE #23

All the labor of man is for his mouth, and yet the appetite is not filled. Better is the sight of the eyes than the wandering of the desire. This also is vanity and a chasing after wind.

ECCLESIASTES 6:7,9

LET'S REFLECT ON THE QUOTE & WRITE YOUR THOUGHTS

QUOTE #24

He who loves silver shall not be satisfied with silver; nor he who loves abundance, with increase: this also is vanity.

ECCLESIASTES 5:10

LET'S REFLECT ON THE QUOTE & WRITE YOUR THOUGHTS

_____

QUOTE #25

There is a grievous evil which I have seen under the sun: wealth kept by its owner to his harm. Those riches perish by misfortune, and if he has fathered a son, there is nothing in his hand.

As he came forth from his mother's womb, naked shall he go again as he came, and shall take nothing for his labor, which he may carry away in his hand.

This also is a grievous evil, that in all points as he came, so shall he go. And what profit does he have who labors for the wind?

All his days are in darkness and mourning, he is frustrated, and has sickness and wrath.

ECCLESIASTES 5:15-17

LET'S REFLECT ON THE QUOTE & WRITE YOUR THOUGHTS

QUOTE #26

Look, this only have I found: that God made man upright; but they search for many schemes.

ECCLESIASTES 7:29

LET'S REFLECT ON THE QUOTE & WRITE YOUR THOUGHTS

_____
_____
_____
_____
_____
_____
_____
_____
_____
_____
_____
_____
_____
_____
_____
_____
_____
_____
_____
_____
_____
_____
_____

QUOTE #27

Who is like the wise man? And who knows the interpretation of a thing? A man's wisdom makes his face shine, and the hardness of his face is changed.

ECCLESIASTES 8:1

LET'S REFLECT ON THE QUOTE & WRITE YOUR THOUGHTS

QUOTE #28

For all this I laid to my heart, even to explore all this: that the righteous, and the wise, and their works, are in the hand of God; whether it is love or hatred, man doesn't know it; all is before them.

ECCLESIASTES 9:1

LET'S REFLECT ON THE QUOTE & WRITE YOUR THOUGHTS

QUOTE #29

If a man fathers a hundred children, and lives many years, so that the days of his years are many, but his soul is not filled with good, and moreover he has no burial; I say, that a stillborn child is better than he.

ECCLESIASTES 6:3

LET'S REFLECT ON THE QUOTE & WRITE YOUR THOUGHTS

QUOTE #30

Dead flies cause the oil of the perfumer to send forth an evil odor; so does a little folly outweigh wisdom and honor.

A wise man's heart is at his right hand, but a fool's heart at his left. Yes also, when the fool walks by the way, his understanding fails him, and he says to everyone that he is a fool.

If the spirit of the ruler rises up against you, do not leave your place; for gentleness lays great offenses to rest.

ECCLESIASTES 10:1-4

LET'S REFLECT ON THE QUOTE & WRITE YOUR THOUGHTS

QUOTE #31

Do not curse the king, no, not in your thoughts; and do not curse the rich in your bedchamber: for a bird of the sky may carry your voice, and that which has wings may tell the matter.

ECCLESIASTES 10:20

LET'S REFLECT ON THE QUOTE & WRITE YOUR THOUGHTS

QUOTE #32

Give a portion to seven, yes, even to eight; for you do not know what evil will be on the earth.

ECCLESIASTES 11:2

LET'S REFLECT ON THE QUOTE & WRITE YOUR THOUGHTS.

QUOTE #33

He who observes the wind won't sow; and he who regards the clouds won't reap.

ECCLESIASTES 11:4

LET'S REFLECT ON THE QUOTE & WRITE YOUR THOUGHTS

QUOTE #34

By slothfulness the roof sinks in; and through idleness of the hands the house leaks.

ECCLESIASTES 10:18

LET'S REFLECT ON THE QUOTE & WRITE YOUR THOUGHTS

_____
_____
_____
_____
_____
_____
_____
_____
_____
_____
_____
_____
_____
_____
_____
_____
_____
_____
_____
_____
_____
_____
_____
_____
_____
_____

WHAT DID YOU THINK ABOUT ECCLESIASTES WITH GOD'S WISDOM

Thank you for purchasing this book. I know you could have picked any number of books to read but you picked this book and for that I am extremely grateful.

I hope it added value & quality to your everyday life. If so, it would be really nice if you could share this book with your friends and family.

If you enjoyed this book and found some benefit in reading it, I'd like to hear from you and hope that you could take some time to post a review.

I want you to know that your review is very important to me.

Thank you again & I wish you all the best as you journey wisely through life.

OTHER BOOKS TO CONSIDER

Proverbs with God's Wisdom: Navigating life wisely with 400+ quotes across 30+ topics from the Biblical book of Proverbs

If you are new to Audible you can get the audiobook version free with a free 30 days Audible trial.

Please follow the below *bit.ly* links based on where you reside.

US: *bit.ly/MLJ_Proverbs_US*

UK: *bit.ly/MLJ_Proverbs_UK*

France: *bit.ly/MLJ_Proverbs_FR*

Germany: *bit.ly/MLJ_Proverbs_DE*

All other countries:
bit.ly/MLJ_Proverbs_Others

Psalms with God's Wisdom: Navigate life wisely with 100+ quotes & proverbs of wisdom, prayer, thanksgiving, trust, praise & worship hymns from the Biblical book of Psalms

If you are new to Audible you can get the audiobook version free with a free 30 days Audible trial.

Please follow the below *bit.ly* links based on where you reside.

US: *bit.ly/MLJ_Psalms_US*

UK: *bit.ly/MLJ_Psalms_UK*

France: *bit.ly/MLJ_Psalms_FR*

Germany: *bit.ly/MLJ_Psalms_DE*

All other countries: *bit.ly/MLJ_Psalms_Others*

Made in the USA
Las Vegas, NV
28 November 2021

35538932R00059